One day Bean was asleep in the little shed. He was dreaming of things to eat.

He was dreaming of six cream buns in his dish. "Yum, yum," he said, "six real cream buns for me to eat."

Then he saw Jelly. She was stealing the cream buns from his dish. She was eating them.

Bean jumped up. He screamed. It was a dream. Jelly was asleep next to him and his dish was not there.

Bean went back to sleep. Zzz .. zzz. Soon he was dreaming again. He was peeping in the hut.

Chuff, the big cat, was having a feast. He was eating fish and chips. "Yum, yum," he said. "What a treat!"

Chuff had two big heaps of fish and chips. He had dishes of peaches and cream. "Yum, yum," he said. "Lots of treats!"

Chuff was eating his big feast.
He let Bean eat a heap of chips.
"Yum, yum," he said. But the feast was not real.

Bean jumped up and screamed. It was a dream. He was in the little shed with Jelly. Chuff was not there.

Bean went to look in his dish. He saw three red beans and a green leaf. "Ugh!" he said. "I will go back to sleep and dream of good things to eat."

"ea"

dream	eat
real	cream
stealing	feast
leaf	treat
screamed	Bean
peaches	heaps

"ee"

asleep	green
peeping	three

High Frequency Words

day in the he of to in for
she up it a and big look cat
was for went

one saw little his him then
from them but next back again
good what two not there had
with jumped